Picture Window Books • Minneapolis, Minnesota

First American edition published in 2004 by
Picture Window Books
5115 Excelsior Boulevard
Suite 232
Minneapolis, MN 55416
1-877-845-8392
www.picturewindowbooks.com

First published in Great Britain by
A & C Black Publishers Limited
37 Soho Square, London W1D 3QZ
Copyright © Two's Company 2003

Printed in the United States of America.

Library of Congress Cataloging-in-Publication Data
Bailey, Jacqui.
Monster bones : the story of a dinosaur fossil / written by
Jacqui Bailey ; illustrated by Matthew Lilly.— 1st American ed.
p. cm. — (Science works)
Summary: Describes how the bones of a dinosaur became
fossilized, were discovered by a paleontologist, and were
ultimately displayed in a museum.
Includes bibliographical references and index.
ISBN 1-4048-0565-6 (Reinforced lib. bdg.)
1. Dinosaurs—Juvenile literature. 2. Fossils—Juvenile
literature. [1. Dinosaurs. 2. Fossils.]
I. Lilly, Matthew, ill. II. Title.
QE861.5 .B34 2004
567.9—dc22   2003020117

For Nick
JB

For Sarah and Peter
ML

3

Millions upon millions of years ago,
a dinosaur wandered by the edge of a river.

ALL I WANT IS
A NICE FAT FISH OR
A JUICY LIZARD.

The dinosaur was
hungry. It hadn't
caught anything
in days.

OH, YES!
MINE, ALL
MINE!

As it stalked through the
bushes, it saw a lizard sitting
on a rock up ahead.

The dinosaur pounced . . . and missed. The rock began to wobble.

It crashed down the riverbank into the water—and the dinosaur went with it.

The dinosaur lay on the riverbed, and all kinds of fish, crabs, and other creatures came to feed on its body.

The soft parts that didn't get eaten rotted away. In the end, all that remained were the dinosaur's teeth and bones.

The gently flowing river water brought sand and mud that covered the bones like a thick blanket.

And there the dinosaur stayed.

9

But as the years went by, something strange happened.

The dinosaur's bones began to turn into stone.

How? Well, it goes something like this: A bone feels smooth and solid, but if you look at it through a microscope, you'll see that the bone is really full of tiny holes.

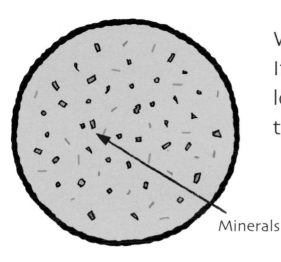

Minerals

Water isn't always what it seems, either. It might look clean and clear, but it can be carrying lots of tiny grains of solid stuff, called minerals, that are too small to see.

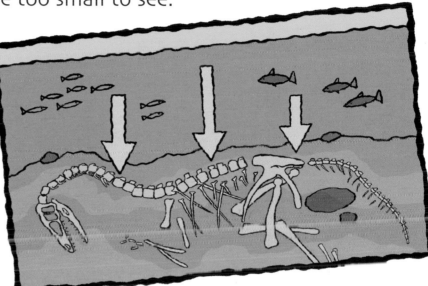

As our dinosaur lay on the riverbed, the river water soaked right through its muddy blanket and into its bones.

The minerals in the water slowly filled up all the holes in the bones.

Parts of the bones rotted away, and the minerals filled up those gaps, too.

Eventually, most of the bony material was replaced by minerals, and the bones had turned into stone.

11

More and more layers of sand and mud piled on top of the dinosaur bones.

Each layer added more weight, which pressed down on the sand and mud underneath until they hardened into rock.

Millions of years went by.

Up above, things changed. The river dried up and disappeared, and all the dinosaurs died.

Grass and trees grew where the river had been, and different kinds of animals wandered around.

Very, very slowly, over the years, the layers of rock were pushed upward.

Did you know that the surface of the Earth is always shifting? Sometimes, over millions of years, huge pieces of land push against each other. As they do, parts of the land can be slowly scrunched up into huge folds—making mountains.

Wind and rain and snow and ice wore away at the layers. The dinosaur bones came closer and closer to the surface.

One wintery afternoon (after a particularly bad rainstorm), two passing hikers noticed an odd-looking stone.

The rain had washed some of the soil away, and the odd-looking stone was sticking out of the ground.

The hikers picked it up and took it home.

They showed it to a friend who worked in a museum. The friend was a paleontologist (PAY-lee-on-TOL-uh-jist).

Paleontologists love odd-looking stones. She got very excited.

THIS ISN'T ANY OLD STONE, IT'S A DINOSAUR FOSSIL!

Fossils are pieces of ancient animals or plants that have (usually) been turned to stone. They may be thousands or even millions of years old.

The word *fossil* comes from the Latin word *fossilis,* which means "dug up."

Fossils are often found buried in rock. Paleontologists are scientists who dig up fossils and study them to find out what life was like a long time ago.

The paleontologist found out where the dinosaur fossil came from and set off with a team of helpers to see if she could discover any more.

THIS IS GOING TO BE GOOD. I CAN FEEL IT IN MY BONES!

The first job was to dig away the top layer of soil to find out how many fossil bones were there.

Then the fossil bones were carefully chipped out of the rock with hammers and chisels. Everyone had to work slowly since fossils are easily broken.

Sometimes the rock surrounding a fossil was scraped away with small knives, and dirt was brushed off with toothbrushes.

The workers used magnifying glasses to help them see where the rock ended and the fossil began.

It took weeks and weeks.

They made lots of notes about where each fossil was found and took tons of photographs.

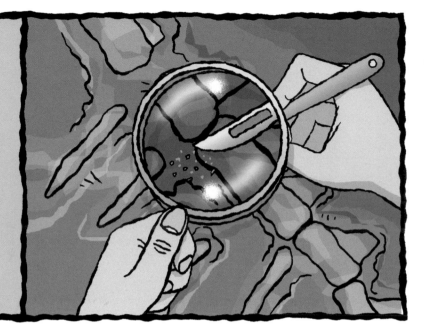

They even drew a map of how the fossils lay together in the ground.

Then each fossil was lifted out of the ground and wrapped up to protect it.

Large fossils were covered with layers of bandages soaked in wet plaster, which dried into hard shells. Smaller fossils were packed in plastic foam and put in boxes.

The workers labeled each fossil to show what it was and where it had been found.

I THINK I'M GOING TO BE SICK!

At last, the fossils were loaded onto a truck and driven off to the museum.

At the museum, the wrapped-up fossil bones were put in a storage room—along with lots of others.

They were all waiting for a scientist to study them. Some fossils had been there for years!

One day, the fossil bones were taken to the museum laboratory. The plaster coverings were cut away, and the fossils were soaked in chemicals to strengthen them.

Then the paleontologist and her team began the long job of chiseling and drilling away bits of rock still left around the fossils. They had to be careful not to chip the fossil itself.

In really tricky places, such as inside the skull, they used dentist's drills, metal toothpicks, and even needles to get the rock out.

THIS IS MORE LIKE IT.

Last of all, they polished the fossil bones until they shined.

Next, the paleontologist took more photos and made careful drawings of the fossil bones.
She would use them in her report when she wrote about the dinosaur and how it was found.

She compared her fossils with ones that had been found before. This helped her figure out what type of dinosaur the fossils belonged to.

HEY! IT'S UNCLE BILLY.

Finally, all the fossil bones were fitted together. It was hard to know which ones went where.

To help them, the paleontologist and her team used the map they'd made and the photographs they'd taken when they dug up the fossils.

The fossil bones were wired together to keep them in place.

Now the fossil dinosaur is on display in the museum. People come from all around to look at it and marvel at an amazing creature that walked the earth 220 million years ago.

Not all fossils are made of stone . . .

FROZEN SOLID

I'LL CATCH MY DEATH OUT HERE.

In the far north, in icy-cold places such as Alaska and Siberia, much of the land is frozen year-round.

Sometimes, plants and animals are buried in ice, and they may stay there for thousands of years.

People have even dug up whole woolly mammoths—skin and all—that died and were frozen 40,000 years ago.

TAR BABIES

Then there are animals that fell into lakes of sticky, black tar.

The lakes formed about a million years ago, when oil from deep below the ground bubbled up to the surface. Rainwater collected on top of the tar, but any animal that tried to drink from the lake got stuck and was sucked down. The tar then stopped the animal's body from rotting away.

Hundreds of whole animal fossils have been found in tar pits, from saber-toothed tigers to frogs.

ALL I WANTED WAS A DRINK OF WATER!

FOREVER AMBER

I GUESS I'M STUCK HERE THEN.

The sticky endings don't stop there. Some pine trees produce a gluey juice called resin. If insects, or even small tree frogs or lizards, walk in the resin, they get stuck and are caught there forever.

As the resin dries, it hardens into a glassy stone called amber. Millions of years later, the amber might be found with a perfect fossil animal still trapped inside it.

BITS AND BLOBS

Sometimes, all a paleontologist finds are fossils of things an animal left behind, such as its eggs or footprints—or even its droppings.

Fossil droppings are called coprolites, and paleontologists like nothing better than digging them up. That's because coprolites contain tiny pieces of ancient food—plants or bits of bone. Scientists study coprolites to find out what sort of food the animal that left the dropping ate. This also tells them what plants or other animals were alive at the same time.

TRY IT AND SEE

LASTING IMPRESSIONS

Some fossils are just copies of something that was once living. Say an animal bone, a shell, or even a leaf becomes trapped in rock.

Strong chemicals called acids may dissolve it, leaving just a shape or impression of it in the rock. If the shape then fills up with a different type of mineral, a copy or model of the original object is made.

Here's how to make some fossil models of your own. Remember to label them!

You will need:
- modeling clay
- thin card and tape
- something to use for your fossil shape —a shell, leaf, small bone, small plastic toy, or even your hand!
- plaster of paris

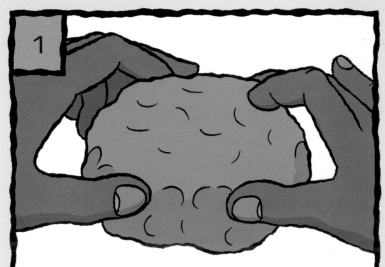

Roll out a piece of modeling clay. It must be thick enough and wide enough for you to press your object into it and have a little space around it.

1 inch

Cut the card into a strip about 1 inch (2 ½ centimeters) wide and long enough to make a circle around your object.

3 Tape the ends of the card circle together, and push it gently into the clay base. Now press your object onto the clay, and then lift it up again. You should be able to see a clear shape or impression of the object in the modeling clay.

4 Mix the plaster of paris into a fairly runny paste, and pour it over the shape until the card circle is about two-thirds full. Then leave it somewhere warm and dry to set.

5 When the plaster is hard, peel away the card and the clay base. Admire your fossil! You can leave it like it is or decorate it any way you like.

FABULOUS FOSSILS

The oldest fossils we know of are about 3,500 MILLION years old! They look like large white circles in the rocks. They were made by the bodies of bacteria— tiny lifeforms that are too small to see just with our eyes. For millions of years, bacteria were the only living things on Earth.

ONCE UPON A TIME, WE RULED THE WORLD, YOU KNOW!

The oldest dinosaur fossils found so far are about 230 million years old. For hundreds of years, people thought dinosaur fossils were the bones of dragons and other magical monsters.

Some fossils aren't even dead! There are a few types of plants and animals in the world that haven't changed at all for millions of years. They are called living fossils, and they look just the same now as their millions-of-times-great-great grandparents did.
    One of the most famous living fossils is a grumpy-looking fish called a coelacanth (*SEE-luh-kanth*). Its relatives first swam the seas 400 million years ago (long before the dinosaurs appeared).

YOU'D BE GRUMPY TOO IF PEOPLE KEPT CALLING YOU A FOSSIL!

INDEX

FACT HOUND

Fact Hound offers a safe, fun way to find Web sites related to this book. All of the sites on Fact Hound have been researched by our staff.

http://www.facthound.com

1. Visit the Fact Hound home page.

2. Enter a search word related to this book, or type in this special code: 1404805656.

3. Click the FETCH IT button.

Your trusty Fact Hound will fetch the best sites for you!